THE LIFE CYCLE LIBRARY

for Young People

The Life Cycle Library

for Young People

Book
3

Published by

PARENT AND CHILD INSTITUTE, CHICAGO

We are indebted to many professional organizations for their help and advice in preparing this set. Among the associations we wish to thank are: American Medical Association, American College of Obstetrics and Gynecology, American Academy of Pediatrics, and National Safety Council.

A NOTE TO READERS

The story told on the following pages is one of the most fascinating and important ones in the life of every human being. Doctors are still trying to unravel the enormous mystery of how a baby comes to be. They are still trying to discover the details of the process by which a tiny cell no larger than a speck of dust grows to be a growing, eating, crying, laughing, loving baby.

The pages that follow present the facts of this story as they are understood today. Distinguished doctors, psychiatrists, educators, and clergymen carefully checked the information presented here, and they have found it accurate. In the pages that follow, you will learn how you came to be, how you fit into the endless cycle of life, and what stages of that cycle lie ahead of you.

A special note to our girl readers

Many times in the pages that follow, the pronoun "he" actually means "he or she." It seemed sort of inhuman to call a baby "it," and it would have gotten rather tiresome to keep saying "he or she" when referring to a baby, so we adopted the standard grammatical practice of using the single pronoun "he." We want our girl readers to know that we value them, too; that we are not showing favoritism to boys.

THE EDITORS

In nearly every article you will find words printed in **bold face.** This special type is a signal that there is a glossary entry on this topic in the fourth volume. If you would like additional information about a word in bold face type, look for it in the alphabetical listing in the glossary.

At the end of many listings in the glossary, you will also find a note that tells you to look for a particular chapter or chapters in the first three volumes for expanded information. For example, after the entry on **birth** in the glossary, there is a note which will tell you that there is an entire chapter discussing birth in Book 2.

CONTENTS

16

YOU
AND YOUR
FAMILY

The most important part of growing up is to learn to become independent. When you were a baby, your parents had to care for you in every way. They made all the decisions for you when you were little. They decided what you would eat, where you would live, where you would go to school, what clothes you would wear, and what religion you would follow.

Over a period of years, you slowly became more independent. You learned how to tie your shoes. Then you were allowed to cross certain streets by yourself. Even before you went to school, you started to learn to be apart from your parents. You learned about life in school, and how to get along with teachers and other students. You learned that you had to finish homework on time. Gradually, over the years, you have become less and less dependent on your parents.

The change from total dependence on your family to independence does not happen overnight. The process of becoming independent sometimes causes moments of uncertainty. Some of these uncertainties occur because your ideas about many things are different from those of your parents. This difference in attitudes is widely referred to as the "generation gap." The term refers not only to the difference in years between parents and their children, but also to the differences in attitudes that exist between them.

The generation gap has always existed, because parents were once children and had parents of their own. When each younger generation begins to grow up and to develop ideas of its own, these ideas are likely to be different from those of the older generation.

Because your parents' ideas may not always agree with your own, you may wonder who is right. Your parents may issue orders about how you should wear your hair, or how you should dress for school. They may tell you about hair styles for young people when they were your age, or how they dressed for school.

This difference between their ideas and yours is something you will learn to live with as you continue growing up. You may not agree with your parents and you may reject their ideas. But just because you reject their ideas doesn't mean you are rejecting them. When they do not agree with what you do, it doesn't mean that they don't love you. They try to guide you to values which they believe are good and worthwhile.

Watching children grow up and develop is a natural and meaningful satisfaction for your parents. You will find this

out when you are a parent. Parents find great joy in watching children learn to speak, to walk, and to do simple chores. You have probably heard your own parents talk about your first spoken words, or something you did in first grade. For years they have made most of the decisions that affected your life. Now they have to turn over more of this decision making to you. It is a tough thing for them to do. They know you have to learn to make your own decisions in order to become adult, but they also know you are not as experienced as they are.

Family life has changed

When your grandfather was a child, family life was vastly different from today. Mothers and fathers had clear duties. Mothers stayed home, cooked, cleaned, and sewed. They spent little time outside the home. It was expected that girls would grow up to be wives and mothers, and do household chores like their mothers. Fathers earned money. Their sons were usually expected to do the same kind of work the father did. Social life was centered around the home. The family joined together in town or church activities.

Now, according to the U.S. Department of Commerce, of a total of more than 25 million working women in the United States, 62 percent are married. These women, unlike their grandmothers, are not home all day long. Many mothers, if they do not work, help charitable organizations. They spend fewer hours at home or with their families than mothers of a generation or more ago.

Parents being away from home isn't felt as much today as it would have been two or three generations ago. Now, young peoples' activities are not centered around the home

as much as they used to be. Instead of the nightly family singing sessions around the old upright piano, there are school choral groups. Scout groups introduce the world of nature to the young person, where previously, learning about wild flowers and trees was something that was done on Sunday outings with the family.

Today's parents tend to see their children as individuals, and usually do not try to fit them into the molds of their own lives. Girls are encouraged to prepare for careers, either before marriage or after their families are raised. Boys are not pressured to follow their fathers' occupations.

Family life has changed, too, in that a lot more is known now about how character and personality develop. Your parents have probably used guidebooks from the time you were an infant to learn how to cope with fevers, rashes, and behavior. Your parents have probably used many books to learn answers to questions concerning your growing up. Modern books stress that much behavior of young people is greatly influenced by environment, or the situation around you. The most significant part of your environment is your family, and family means brothers and sisters as well as parents.

Brothers and sisters are an important part of your environment because they put you into close contact with other young people. Rivalry between brothers and sisters is natural. It would be most unusual if you and your brothers or sisters never argued with each other. It is natural to become angry at someone younger or smaller than yourself, to feel jealous about someone older or smarter than yourself.

You can learn important lessons in getting along with others from family quarrels. Possessions and friends must be shared in a family in a way that is duplicated throughout life. When you grow up and earn your own living, property

must be shared and used by co-workers in ways similar to sharing toys when you are young.

Your parents had an environment when they were young, too. The environment in which they grew up influences the way they act toward you and the rest of your family.

Understanding your parents' attitudes

If you think about your parents' backgrounds, you may be able to understand why some of their attitudes are different from yours. Some of their behavior may stem from their own childhood experiences. For instance, their ways of expressing love were probably developed when they were very young. Parents' ways of showing affection are often based on the ways affection was shown to them when they were children. In

earlier days, it wasn't common for children to see parents kissing each other, or openly kissing their children. Often, persons brought up this way do not show affection easily. But this does not mean that they do not love their children.

Showing favoritism toward one child in a family may have roots in the fact that one or both of your parents came from a family where girls or boys or older or younger children were favored. They may react in an opposite or similar direction with you and your sisters and brothers.

Some parents seem to want to dominate. Perhaps they aren't happy about the way things have gone in their lives. They may feel that they missed out on what they would have liked to do or be. Parents who feel this way may insist that their children do what they did not do. A mother who always

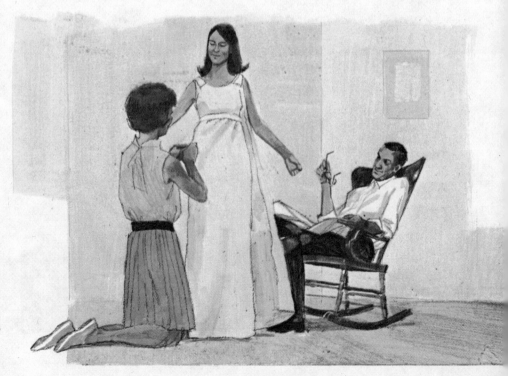

wanted to be a ballet dancer may insist that her daughter take ballet lessons.

Perhaps your parents grew up in a family where lack of money caused many hardships. They want to be sure that this doesn't happen to you. Whether you like it or not, they may try to see that you have advantages they missed.

Some parents who were not as outstanding as their brothers or sisters may wish to have outstanding children. This is possibly part of the reason why your parents may encourage you toward better work, better grades, and entrance into better schools. Of course, parents always want you to do your very best, because they know that will make it possible for you to feel pride in your accomplishments.

Some parents overwhelm children with gifts and privileges. Such behavior may grow out of their never having had enough when they were young. Some parents are unable to express affection even though they want to. They may use gifts to show their affection for their children.

Growing up and preparing your parents for the time when you are mature and will be on your own takes continual understanding and acceptance of both of your sets of values.

When your parents order you to come home from a party earlier than you think you should leave, find out what worries

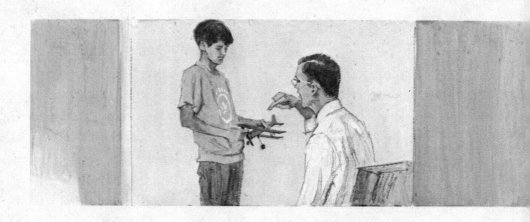

them. Your willingness to tell them frankly and honestly what goes on at a party may relieve some of their worries. Or, you may volunteer to phone them if you want to stay longer than they asked. Taking the time to relieve their worries shows them that you are thoughtful and responsible.

Friends, boys and girls

Some parents hate to see children growing up. When parents see a romantic attachment close at hand, they know that a child is maturing and growing out of the family circle.

Studies show that most parents of today feel inadequate to talk about sex to their children. While their intentions may be good, they have difficulty in bringing themselves to discuss it. This difficulty is caused by the age in which your parents grew up. Even thirty years ago, sex was a forbidden subject in most homes. No education was given in most schools about sexual maturation. When your grandparents and perhaps parents were young, the regular pattern, particularly for girls, was to know little, if anything, about sex before they married.

Because your parents may have had no one with whom to discuss these matters openly when they were young, they

258

feel uncomfortable in talking about them with you. If you let them know that you want them to talk with you, and that you want to hear their viewpoints, you make communicating with them about sex easier.

Parents aren't perfect, either

When you were very young, you probably thought that your parents were the most outstanding people in the world. You may have thought your father was the strongest man in the world, and your mother was the most beautiful woman. But as you got older, you realized that parents can be irritable, impatient, and even unfair. You found that parents do not always behave consistently. Because parents are people, too, they have imperfections. Realizing that parents aren't perfect either is part of the growing up process.

As you were growing up, you probably noticed that if your father was angry about something that occurred during his working day, he might behave irritably when he came home. Sometimes parents relieve their anger at outside situations by being grumpy at home. Psychologists say that it is probably better to show occasional anger than to keep this strong feeling bottled up inside.

Sometimes youngsters see the results of friction between their parents in angry, irritable behavior. Family life is not always smooth. Crises do occur. These are part of the realities of life.

Family crises can affect the way parents treat you, but they do not basically change the fact that your parents love you, and want you to grow up to be a responsible, independent person. Stress that is created at these unfortunate times is usually only temporary, and it is important to realize that adjustments need to be made by all family members. The best thing that you can do in times of crisis is to keep calm yourself and try to help if your assistance is necessary.

Part of growing up usually involves facing one kind of crisis or another within the family. One such crisis may be financial. If a father loses his job, and is out of work for some time, the children are bound to be affected. Their allowances will be cut, and there will be less money for food and clothing. This situation happened to a boy named Jon when he was 12. He realized that as a member of the family team, he had to help out. He helped the owner of a local grocery store unload stock when it was delivered each week, and he earned more

money than his allowance had been. He shared the extra money with his two younger brothers.

When Susan was 13, her father had a serious accident and had to be in the hospital for six months. Susan had little money for clothes. With her mother's help, she learned to sew well enough to make many of her own clothes, which became the envy of her friends because of their styles and fabrics.

Sometimes a parent dies. At first there is a very deep sense of loss and grief. But it is important to remember that life will go on, even though the parent is gone. The child must do what he can to make life happier for himself and for other members of the family.

Amy was 13 when her father died. After the first shock and sadness lessened, Amy's mother took a part-time job during afternoons and early evenings. Amy arranged her schedule to finish classes at three o'clock and then come home to take care of her three younger brothers and sisters. Later, when her mother could stay home again, Amy's experience with her own family made her a popular neighborhood babysitter.

Another crisis some families face is mental illness. One of every five families in the United States is stricken at some time or another by mental illness. Mental illness is treatable, and

a mentally ill person should not be held responsible for what he does. Other members of the family should try to make the sick person know that they understand his illness, and that they love him as much as ever.

Many young people must face a divorce between their parents at a time when they feel they particularly need the love and guidance of both parents. If yours is a divorced family, regardless of which parent you live with, you can be sure that the other loves you just as much as when you all lived together.

Nancy was ten when she began to realize that her parents had stopped loving each other. She was very unhappy listening to her parents argue, and watching the changes in their behavior. They were irritable most of the time, but she understood that they weren't angry at her. They argued a lot, and could never agree on anything.

Finally, Nancy's father moved away, and her parents were divorced. Her father came to visit her every Sunday. She still had both her mother and her father discussing her activities with her, suggesting school projects, and giving her ideas for the craft projects she supervised in a Brownie troop. Nancy knew that both of her parents still loved her. She knew that even though her father was not always present in the home, she could still count on him, as well as her mother, to help her when needed.

Days and sometimes years of crisis occur within families. Yet, somehow, out of each family, young people do grow up and raise their own families. Your life within your family is preparing you for your own future family situation.

Growing up includes learning to accept the fact that your parents' views will continue to be different from yours. Growing up means understanding that your parents behave the way they do not only because they love you but because of the ways in which they were brought up. And, unfortunately, growing up also means recognizing that crises may occur at any time within a family, and learning to meet those crises in a mature way if they should occur.

Of all the friendships you ever make, the most valuable friends you will ever have are your parents. No matter what your differences of opinion are while you are young, there will always be a very real basis for friendship. This basis is a solid foundation of closeness, sharing, and love. When you are grown-up and living on your own, that friendship can take on even another dimension. It can be enriched by the merging of the outlooks and values of adults of two generations.

17

HOW TO KEEP A CONVERSATION GOING

Conversation is an adventure in the give and take of ideas, knowledge, and feelings among people. It can also be a passport into the world of new friendships.

Being able to carry on interesting conversations with people of all ages and types is an art, but it can be learned. The recipe for good conversation, as for a cake, has many ingredients. Three of the most important are simple courtesy, honesty, and oddly enough, listening.

Courtesy is simply a matter of giving others a chance to "speak their piece." Everyone should have the right to ex-

press his own ideas. Also, since they just might be right, it is only fair to let them say what they have to say. The extra spoonful of courtesy that sweetens any conversation is the ability to disagree without being disagreeable.

Courtesy is particularly important in conversation with parents, because there is often disagreement over what you want to do and what they are willing to allow you to do. By hearing what they have to say, you give yourself a chance to honestly examine and to try to understand their reasons. Even if you lose the round, you gain some ground, simply by showing you are willing to listen. Being disagreeable and fighting back is like building a concrete wall between you.

Listening, *really* listening, whether to your parents, friends or strangers, is also a way of learning what makes others tick. How others think and feel, what they believe in and why, are clues which help you understand all kinds of people. Attentive listening is important. The secret is in the timing, in knowing what to say, and how and when to say it.

Without the other important ingredient, honesty, the conversational cake is likely to fall flat. Saying, "I don't know," when you honestly don't know the answer to a question, is easier and safer than pretending to have all the answers.

It sounds simple enough to bake a conversational cake, but almost everyone has those terrible tongue-tied moments when it seems the only possible thing to do is to stare out the window or up at the sky.

Conversation can suddenly fall flat in many situations: on a date, when meeting people for the first time, while talking on the telephone, or in an adults-only group. Often, you *know* how you feel and what you want to say, but how do you get the words out when your throat seems to be glued shut? Why do you feel tongue-tied?

Part of the reason is shyness, a natural feeling almost everyone has at some time. Shyness is the reason why you probably feel at times that you would rather stay in your room with a book than face new people and try to think of what to talk about. When you have that feeling, it is probably because you are thinking so hard about yourself and what you *should* say that you freeze and find it hard to say anything.

One way to overcome this feeling is to take the "I" out of your thinking and to realize that the person you are with may be feeling exactly the same way. After all, the boy, girl, or adult you are speaking to is just another person, someone you can become interested in if you try.

What to talk about

Topics for conversation are all around. With your good friends, it is probably very easy to find much to talk about—school projects, the trouble you are having with a particular subject, teachers, or how the school team is doing.

With strangers or adults, conversation may not be as easy. Usually, however, most people are interested in general topics

such as cars, sports, hobbies, movies, books, television programs, and so on. The main thing is to try to find a topic which interests the other person, ask him a question to get him started, and then let him talk as much as he likes.

The daily newspaper is often a gold mine for good conversational material. A front-page item about space exploration, for instance, can be a springboard to a discussion about whether the United States should spend billions of dollars to explore the solar system. If someone says "No," but you think "Yes," and say so, others will speak their opinions, and the question sets off a lively discussion. In fact, the newspaper is packed with all kinds of conversational topics. All you have to do is read it to find them, then ask others what they think. Know what *you* think too, though. Good listeners are always popular, but you should say what you think.

Where have you been lately? What have you done? These topics are also conversation starters. Remember, however, to just tell the highlights. Suppose you got caught in a tropical storm while on a vacation in Florida, or got lost while on a summer trip, or visited a famous restaurant. Such highlights will be interesting to listeners; what you did every moment of every day will not.

The ordinary everyday things you do, or the ways you spend your free time, can provide conversational topics, also. Your hobbies, club projects, volunteer work, and after school jobs may be of more interest to other people than you think.

Compliments are part of conversation, too. If you honestly feel that a girl friend's new hair style is sensational, or that a boy you know looks terrific in his new turtle-neck sweater, say so, but do not go on and on and on. Sometimes, people *do* get too gushy about paying compliments, even when they mean them. Most people prefer hearing the short, sweet kind.

Only the sincere compliment has any value however, so it is best not to say someone looks great when you really think he or she looks terrible. A good rule to follow about giving compliments is that if you cannot *honestly* say something nice, say nothing. Insincere compliments are not liked by anyone.

On the other hand, if someone compliments you, a smile and a simple "Thank you," is all you need to reply. To protest that you really do not deserve the compliment makes the person feel foolish for having bothered to say something nice.

Conversational tips

Jokes made at someone else's expense, crude or off-color jokes, and very personal questions seldom make good conversation.

Pointing out that Wally's teeth make him look like a gopher, even if they do, may get a big laugh, but the laugh is not worth the price of losing Wally as a friend. Laughter at someone else's expense is a sure way of losing friends.

Telling off-color jokes may give you the center of the stage for a few moments, but why run the risk of offending even

those who might laugh? Most people find these jokes embarrassing, even if they pretend otherwise. Swearing and foul language also have no place in good conversation.

Almost everyone finds the very personal question embarrassing. "How much money does your father make?" or "How much did that dress cost?" are questions better left unasked. If someone asks you such a question, one good way to get out of answering it is to just smile and say, "I hope you don't mind, but I would rather not talk about that."

Unfortunately, it is easy to fall into the "tell all" trap, because most people have a tendency to talk too much and too long about a subject which interests them. Experienced lecturers know that one of the secrets of success is to leave the audience wanting to hear more. The same idea applies to conversation with others. It is better to save something to talk about next time.

No one agrees with everyone *all* the time. This is good; differing viewpoints are the spice of good conversation. How do you disagree without being disagreeable? One way is by "speaking your piece" in a matter-of-fact way, without stepping on a soap box to do it. Another way is by using words such as "I believe," or "I think," then saying quietly and firmly what you do believe or think. Both of these are positive ways of presenting an opposite viewpoint, and they do not imply that the other person is an idiot or a liar.

Practically everyone has committed a conversational error by making a thoughtless or tactless remark without realizing,

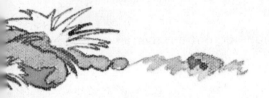

until too late, that someone was hurt or offended. If you find that you have made such a remark, apologize quickly and sincerely. Those two little words, "I'm sorry," go a long way toward taking the sting out of what you have said. Apologizing can save a friendship which might otherwise be lost.

Using the telephone

The telephone is a particularly important part of conversational life. Using it calls for both courtesy and good manners.

When you answer the phone you can simply say "Hello." Then if the call is for you but the caller does not recognize your voice, the correct response is, "This is she," or "This is Nancy." If the call is for someone else, all you need to say is, "Just a moment, please, I'll call her." Since the call is not for you, it is impolite to ask who the caller is, unless the person being called asks you to do so. If the person called is not at home, the polite response is, "I am sorry, she is not here now. Would you care to leave a message?" Keep a pad and pencil handy near the phone, be sure to write the message down, double check what you have written with the caller, and deliver the message as soon as possible.

If the caller has reached the wrong number and apologizes, as most people do, all you need say is "All right." It is both unnecessary and rude to crack the caller's eardrum by slamming the receiver back in place. However, should you reach a wrong number, remember that you have disturbed someone unnecessarily. It is only polite to say, "I am sorry, I have the wrong number."

When you reach the right number, but not the person you are calling, simply ask, "May I speak to Janet, please?" And

when Janet comes to the phone, avoid the "guess who?" routine; tell her immediately who you are.

If you're expecting a call, stay near the phone so that you can answer it yourself, but don't take it for granted that it *is* your call when the phone rings. Give the person on the other end of the line a chance to respond before coming on strong with "Hi, Georgie-boy!" The caller just might be your elderly uncle who may not appreciate being called Georgie-boy.

Just as there is a time and place for doing most things, there is also a right and wrong time to make telephone calls. Usually, you should not call people before 9:00 a.m. or after 10:00 p.m. Tell your friends the best times for you to take calls, and ask them what times are best for them. Knowing when to call will keep you from breaking any "house rules" regarding use of the telephone.

Although the telephone is a great means of communication, it can also create problems between you and other family members if you make too many phone calls or stay on the phone too long. Tying up the telephone when others are trying to sleep, read, or at a time when the family has guests can be a source of irritation. Explain the situation briefly, and ask if you may return the call at a more convenient time.

Since most telephones are shared by the family, certain basic courtesies are expected, and should be observed. Some families put a three-minute limit on calls in order to keep the line free for incoming calls, and to give others in the family a chance to use the phone.

Should girls call boys?

In one high school poll, the majority of boys said they did not like girls to call them. They felt it made the girls seem "pushy," and their families sometimes teased them about the girls who called, something they definitely did not like.

There are times, however, when a girl really has to call a boy. She may have to, for example, invite him to a party she is giving, or she may want to check on an important class assignment due the next day. Most boys do not mind receiving a necessary call from a girl.

At times, you will find while talking to someone on the phone that you have said all you wanted to say. Instead of trying desperately to think of something else to say, it is best to end the conversation simply and courteously with a few words such as, "It was nice of you to call. See you soon," or "I have enjoyed talking with you. Goodbye for now."

As with other types of conversations, the successful telephone conversation begins with courtesy, offers interesting topics, and ends on a short, friendly note.

Talking with adults

The same basic formula for good conversation—courtesy, honesty, and listening—is a bridge into the adult world you will soon be part of. Your first step across that bridge begins with forming the talking-listening habit with your parents, adult relatives, and other adults, including your parents' friends.

Talking to your parents and other adults often seems much more difficult than talking with friends and others of your own age. One reason is simply that it is easier to share your secret hopes, fears, and dreams with your best friends because they have similar feelings. You feel they will understand you, but will your parents?

The answer is usually "yes" because, although you may find it hard to believe, your parents had to cross the same bridge in the same way you do. The kind of understanding you would like *from* them comes through sharing your experiences and thoughts *with* them. If you open the door and let them in, you will find that parents can be the greatest audience in the world. Whether you are an only child or one of ten children in the family, your parents *are* interested in you and in what you think and do.

The old saying that "a girl's best friend is her mother" holds a lot of truth, particularly where romance is involved.

After all, a mother has already gone through the dating, court-
ship, and marriage stages. The girl who is willing to share her
thoughts and feelings about a wonderful new romance, or
to talk about her problems with her current boy friend, often
discovers that her mother can give her valuable suggestions.

A boy might feel better talking to his father about similar
subjects, but if his dad is away a lot, he should not overlook
the fact that his mother can also help him with questions he
has. Because she is a woman, she knows how girls expect boys
to act, and can suggest what he should do.

True, sometimes parents are too busy to stop for the chat
you want to have. It is up to you then to keep trying to get
through to them, perhaps by choosing a quiet time to bring
up what you want to discuss. Making the effort to communi-
cate with your parents is like investing in stocks—it can pay a
lot of dividends, either immediately or over a period of time.

At times your parents will seem too busy to listen, in spite
of the effort you make to get a conversation going. You will
probably feel that you will never be able to corner them long
enough to talk. It pays not to overlook other members of the
family who can and will take the time to talk with you. You
might be surprised to discover that a favorite aunt or uncle,
or even one of your grandparents, has young ideas and understands young people.

Sometimes you don't want to hear your parent's viewpoint
on a particular subject because deep down you know what

276

you want to do is forbidden. There is no law that says you will always like, or must like everything you hear, whether it comes from your parents, friends, or other adults. Once again, however, it is simple courtesy to let them have the chance to "speak their piece."

Two sides of a coin are always different, but they both represent the total value of the coin. Although ideas and viewpoints vary from one generation to the next, basic values do not. What your parents and other adults have to say is your best guide as to what will be expected of you from society.

Part of the difficulty in getting the conversational ball rolling with adults is that it is sometimes hard to see that parents are people, too, although they wear the special labels of Mom and Dad. Though different from yours, they also have hopes, dreams, and fears. The problems they have to solve are different, too, but you all live together in the same world. Every conversation between you and your parents helps each of you to understand the other's viewpoint a little better.

The same thing is true with other adults. They may honestly want to talk with you, but, in spite of their experience and in spite of the fact that they once were the same age as you now, they know there is a difference between you. They may never have heard the hit record that you think is the greatest. Even if they have heard it, they probably do not appreciate it as deeply as you do. They may not know about the ball players or the TV or movie stars you admire. That does not mean they do not understand your feelings.

When they were your age, today's adults had their own hit records. They felt as strongly about them as you feel about yours today. They still like to listen to tunes that were their favorites when they were young. These tunes probably sound as weird to you as your favorites sound to them.

Tastes change and values change. These changes are mostly responsible for the "generation gap."

These changes, however, are like the surface ripples on a deep lake. Beneath the surface are deeper waters that are still and calm. Ernestine Schumann-Heink, a famous German opera singer, had sons who fought on opposite sides during World War I. Late in her life she said, "The forces that bring people together are finer and stronger than the forces that drive them apart." The deeper waters are more important than the surface ripples.

One of the most important forces that brings people together is conversation. Even though your tastes and values may seem to you to be vastly different from those of adults, there is still much that you have in common. You can discover these common bonds through conversation.

Conversation is a way of knowing people better, whether those people be friends, strangers, parents, or other adults. Conversation is your passport to exploring the wider world of different ideas, thoughts and feelings. Most times, this journey begins with a simple "Hello."

18

DATING
FOR GIRLS

In today's world, girls start to date when they are fairly young—generally in their early teens. There is no "right" age to begin dating; it depends upon a number of factors. Just as some girls mature physically earlier than others, some mature sooner socially.

Some girls are entirely comfortable about attending group social events with a particular boy when they are still in grade school. Those who feel less comfortable about boy-girl relationships may not have a first date until the sophomore year in high school, and sometimes later than that. Then too, some parents are agreeable to early dating—other parents prefer that their children wait until high school to begin dating.

Whenever a girl "discovers" boys, she will probably begin to dream about and hope for that first date. She's apt to be both happy and a bit scared, wondering if she'll know what to say and do when the big moment arrives. This doubt is natural; no one is born knowing how to be a good date and everyone learns to be at ease through various dating experiences.

"First" dates are usually invitations to some specific group function such as a boy-girl party given by a friend, school social get-togethers, dances, sports events, or family picnics and outings. One or more adults are generally present at group events. Such dates are a good way of wading into the social swim, because the success of the date doesn't depend on the girl or the boy having to plan what to do; that's already decided. And since everyone will be doing the same thing, it's an easy and comfortable way to have a good time.

Later, dates might include three or four couples who decide to spend an evening together bowling or at the movies. Maybe a boy and girl will double-date with one other couple.

"Double" your fun

Double-dating can be more fun and make for a livelier evening than single-dating. For one thing, a four-way conversation is often easier to keep going. Everyone is more comfortable in the social situation together than either couple might be as a twosome. Double-dating is also a convenient way of arranging for transportation if only one car is available.

It is usually the boy who suggests doubling, and a double-date should be planned so both couples know what they will be doing. It's a good idea for all four to talk over plans together to avoid misunderstanding about time and place. The

girls can check with each other about where they are going and what to wear.

Double-dating is likely to be more fun if you double with a couple who have the same kind of rules about such things as the time for getting home, the places you're allowed to go, and what you're allowed to do.

Sooner or later, a girl graduates to single-dating, when she and a boy go out as a twosome. By the time she has worked up to this "just us" type of evening, she's had time to acquire some of the social skills.

What makes a great date?

Every girl wants to be attractive to boys. While it's true that an especially pretty girl may be asked out more, being "datable" depends on things other than just good looks.

One group of high school boys who were asked what they especially liked and disliked about girls agreed that enthusiasm was much more important than beauty. They liked the girl who was fun to be with—who had a good time whether the occasion was a prom or a ping-pong game.

As a popular song puts it, "I enjoy being a girl." The boys said they liked girls who acted like girls, not tomboys. They liked girls who were friendly but not "pushy." They especially liked the girl who had a good sense of humor and tried to see the amusing side of things, even if a date did not work out as planned. Also among things the boys admired were the kind of good looks that come from good grooming and neatness.

Being "neat" means looking more than just clean and combed. It means avoiding weird fads in hairdos, makeup, and dress. The best-dressed girl isn't necessarily the one who has a closet full of clothes; she's the girl who has studied herself and various clothing styles to learn what looks best on her.

Clean, shining hair and carefully kept hands and nails are basic to good grooming. A minimum of makeup, applied prop-

erly and sparingly, will accentuate natural good looks. The rule is: use less for daytime than evening; less for school than parties; and never, never, apply makeup in public.

Being attractive also includes avoiding certain unattractive actions such as loud, shrieking laughter, top-of-the-voice comments, and catty remarks about other girls. Remember to sit and stand tall at all times—a "slouch" may look so tired that a boy would fear she'd fall asleep on a date.

When he asks you

When that one special boy finally asks you to go to a party or a movie, how should you act? First, any boy who asks for a date has a right to expect a definite answer, and not a maybe-yes, maybe-no stalling routine. If you have to check with your folks before accepting, tell the boy so, and say that you'll let him know tomorrow or the day after.

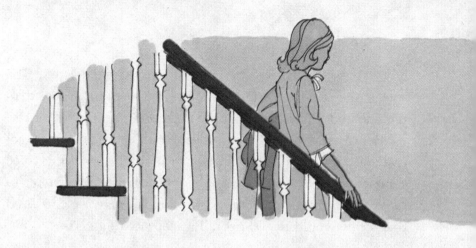

Once you've said yes, keep your word and don't break the date even if someone comes along with a better offer. If the second boy is really interested, he'll ask again, but if you break the date with the one you accepted first, you'll soon become known as a "date-breaker."

Have a happy time

A few guidelines on how to act will help pave the way for a smooth evening. First, when your date comes to get you, be ready to answer the door yourself. The female who is never ready on time may be the cartoonist's pet, but she's loved by nobody else. Have your date come into your home—no sitting out in the car and leaning on the horn until you show up. Introduce him to your parents. They will carry on the conversation while you get your coat. Tell your folks where you're going and that you'll be home at a certain time. This lets the boy know when you have to be home.

Wait for your date to open the car door and say "thank you." If it's a movie date, stand to one side while he buys the tickets. Once inside, you follow the usher down the aisle and go to your seat first. Wait for your date to ask if you'd like

popcorn or candy—maybe his budget won't cover it. Afterwards, wait for him to suggest having a snack, for the same reason. When he does, be considerate of the state of his wallet by asking him what he's going to order. His answer will clue you as to whether it's a steakburger deluxe or "just-a-coke-please" evening, and you act accordingly.

If you do go to a restaurant, you follow the headwaiter or hostess to the table. He or she will hold your chair and help you out of your coat. Put your purse and gloves in your lap, even on the floor, anywhere but on the table. After you've decided what you want to eat, tell your date. He gives the waiter your order, then his.

When it's time to say goodnight, keep it brief. Tell your date how much you've enjoyed the evening—something like, "It was such fun to be with you" or "It really was a great evening. Goodnight." Even if you have time to spare until cur-few, avoid prolonging the conversation. Why? Well, if you leave a boy wishing he could spend more time in your company, he's bound to ask you out again soon, isn't he?

What about a goodnight kiss? A majority of girls (and boys, too) agree that a first date is too soon for goodnight kissing. Girls, particularly, usually want time to know a boy better before deciding whether they like him well enough to kiss him. Even then, most girls consider that a goodnight kiss is a special way of saying affectionately, "You're nice" or "I like being with you."

With some boys you may find lots of things to talk about; with others, you might not. When you're at a loss for words, a few interested questions about your date's likes, dislikes, and special interests will help get the conversation going again. And after you ask, *listen.* Every male is flattered to find a girl who wants to hear him talk.

Refusing a date

Some girls have difficulty saying "no" to a date they can't or don't want to accept and some will say "yes" only to the boy who is tall, handsome, or a good dancer. They would rather stay home than go out with a boy who doesn't fit their picture of an ideal date. It's a mistake to assume that because a boy

doesn't qualify in the good looks or dance department, he can't be fun and someone good to know.

The girl who refuses a date because a boy is too short or has a big nose or for some other equally unimportant reason really limits her dating chances. She can even lower them to zero. More important, she misses the chance to find out what different boys are like.

If the boy is, however, someone you really don't want to date because his personality simply grates on you or because he has a terrible reputation, the kindest thing to do is to give him absolutely no encouragement. The "some other time" response amounts to leading the boy on in the hope that you'll eventually say "yes," and that's unfair. If you are simply not interested in him, refuse his attentions (any and all of them) with courtesy, firmness, and finality.

When you've refused a date as nicely as possible, it isn't necessary to give a long explanation of your reasons. If the boy comes right out and asks, "Why not?" just repeat that you have other plans and change the subject.

Once in a while a girl gets "stood up," which is always embarrassing and annoying. There you are—all dressed up and no place to go. What to do about it? First give the boy a chance to explain. There may have been some misunderstanding about time or place, or some other valid reason why he didn't show up. Give him the benefit of the doubt. If it turns out that he was simply a no-show, that's your cue to refuse the next time he asks for a date.

How to chase him till he catches you

When a girl sets her sights on a certain boy who seems too shy to ask for a date, what can she do to get him interested? You can be friendly and pleasant without appearing to chase him by simply smiling and saying "Hi" whenever you see him. This helps the boy feel that you might be easy to talk to. If you attend some of the same classes, ask him a question about an assignment before class begins, or leave the room when he does and make some casual comment.

Another approach is to get a girlfriend to invite him to her house for some *real* reason, such as forming a new club. Or a boy who is a buddy may invite him to join your gang for a snack after school.

It may take a while to break through the barrier of a boy's shyness, but with patience, this kind of low-key approach can lead into easy conversation about casual things. After a period of time, the boy should feel more comfortable about talking to

you. From there, it isn't such a big step to talking about something it would be fun to do together.

If after several weeks, however, there is no response to all your friendly overtures (some boys are too immature and uneasy around girls to become friendly, or are just not interested), it's better to forget that project and concentrate on a more approachable boy.

What if you don't want to be caught?

Quite the opposite of the shy boy who finds it hard even to say hello is the too-eager-beaver who thinks that every girl he dates owes him the chance to improve his kissing technique. To such boys dating is a game, and some even admit they try to get a necking session going simply to find out if the girl "will" or "won't." The girl who goes along with the game is apt

291

to end up with a not-so-nice name. That kind of boy builds himself up by boasting to his buddies about how many times he makes out.

How do you handle the boy who moves too fast too soon without going into a deep-freeze act? The smart girl develops a technique of her own—she moves away quickly and slips out of reach with a smiling shake of her head, or saying, "Sorry, not now." The key word is "quickly." No fair going along with things until your date is all excited, then acting indignant!

How does a girl know if the boy is just playing games? Easy—he tries the same routine on every date. If that's the case, scratch him off the list. After all, any good date should mean mutually shared fun and pleasure—not just fun for one. It's the girl who makes the rules. You don't have to play this kind of game to be popular, and the boy who really likes you will respect your no-necking rule.

It's a good idea to set up a few rules about home dates, too. First of all, make sure one of your parents will be present. Not on the scene, of course, but just *there*, somewhere.

292

Keep the lights on and the door to the room open so there's no question about what's going on inside. This eliminates giving the boy the idea that he's been invited to a necking session. Have something special to do—set up a checkerboard, or have some new records out, or bake brownies.

Going steady

Some time during the dating years, the big question comes up—should you or should you not go steady? As with everything else in life, there are some good and some not-so-good points to think about.

One positive factor is, of course, that going steady is a form of social security for a girl—she doesn't have to worry about having dates every weekend, or finding an escort for the prom and other important social events. But once a girl agrees to date one boy exclusively, she has to play fair. If her steady can't take her to something special, she stays home—alone.

Every girl enjoys the special feeling of being a boy's one-and-only, knowing she comes first with him. He'll plan things that are especially interesting to her, and take her to places she most enjoys. She knows she can depend on him; she feels that they share a special togetherness.

That wonderful "just we two" feeling can have a negative side, though. Some couples think so much about being together they can't think about anything else. As a result, school work suffers—a fact that makes parents justifiably unhappy. If a boy and girl drift into doing too many things alone, their mutual friends are apt to drift away. Then there's the question of sex. Young people who are very frequently together and who feel very close to each other may not be able to handle their strong feelings of physical attraction for each other.

Although a girl may believe that a certain boy is her one and only love and always will be, it does not often work out that way during the early dating years. This is true simply because during these years friendships and interests change quickly. Breaking up can be a heartbreaking experience for a girl, especially if she feels jilted. This puts a big dent in her pride, and because everything reminds her of *him,* she finds it hard to fill the emptiness in her life.

Even when a girl waits until her later teens to go steady, she sometimes discovers after a few months that the boy bores her and that the magic of doing everything together is gone. Then she has the problem of how to tell him he's no longer special without hurting *his* feelings.

The many girls who have traveled the road from going steady to early marriage to quick divorce and then back to playing the field know it is all an unhappy experience. An important part of growing up is learning about the world and about the many different kinds of people who make it interesting. The high school and college years are the time when a girl has the freedom to share and compare her ideas and views of the world with many other people, including members of the male sex. A girl who ties herself down early to one of the first boys with whom she has something in common will miss the greatest opportunity she will ever have to develop an understanding of others.

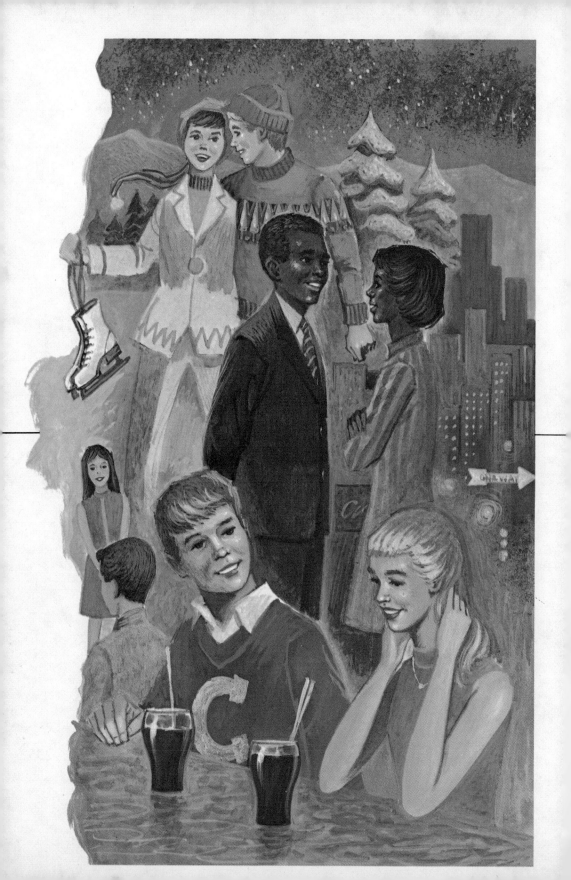

19

DATING
FOR BOYS

When does a boy start thinking about dating? The age varies, just as it does with girls. Some boys start at age 13, but others are neither interested in, nor interesting to, girls until later.

Generally, though, sometime during the early teen years, a boy graduates from the all-girls-are-pests class. The idea one day hits him that he would like to walk that cute girl from class home. When he does, he takes the first step into the boy-girl social world. He discovers that being with girls and having them for friends can be fun. Sooner or later, he thinks about taking one certain girl to some particular event. But his first big question is how to ask a girl for a date. Wondering how to ask the first time can be a problem for a boy.

Practically every boy is nervous the first time he asks for a date. Most find it hard to work up their courage. Even when they really want to ask a girl for a date, boys usually think of a lot of reasons for not asking. They are sure the girl will say "no," that she likes someone else better, or that she really wouldn't want to go to the party with him, anyway.

The truth is, however, that a girl likes being noticed, and asking her for a date is the best way of telling her she is noticed. Once a boy realizes this, it isn't so hard for him to find the courage to ask. Of course, knowing how to ask increases the chances of getting a "yes" answer.

Some boys can't quite do the asking face-to-face the first time; they feel more comfortable using the telephone. But whether personally or by telephone, the first rule is to ask a girl for a date at least a week in advance. Girls don't like being called at 7:30 to do something at 8:00 that evening.

No girl likes to admit she doesn't have a date, so how you phrase your invitation is important, too. It is better not to ask, "Are you busy tomorrow night?" or, "What are you doing Friday night?" Instead, be specific about what you have in mind—a movie, swimming, bowling, a party, or a school dance. You can say, "Will you go to a movie with me Saturday afternoon?" This gives the girl a reason for saying yes or no (maybe she hates movies). It also lets her know what she should wear. A girl will dress differently for a movie than for a picnic. If, happily, she says "yes," tell her the definite time you will pick her up. If for some reason you'll be meeting each other somewhere else, agree on a definite time and place.

If her reply is, "I'll let you know later," give her a chance to do so. Some parents are more strict than others, and she might have to check at home first.

Your first date

Where you go and what you do on that first date depends a lot upon how much money you have to spend. Some of the items a boy is expected to pay for on a date include transportation (bus or cab), dance fees, or tickets to the movies, theater, or sports event. The boy is also expected to pay for popcorn, candy, or cold drinks if at a movie or theater; snacks afterward; and flowers, if it is a formal dance.

It is a good idea to check the state of your wallet first, then invite the girl to do one or two things you can afford. Going to the movies at a neighborhood theater is generally a safe suggestion for a first date. There are lots of other things to do that do not cost much; for example, most sports events, roller skating, a game of tennis, or a school affair.

Because girls usually mature socially before boys do, they expect a boy to behave in certain ways on a date. One survey showed that girls turned thumbs down on the boy who was careless about his appearance, was thoughtless, disrespectful, loud, or a showoff. The girls also said they disliked the boy who tells off-color stories, criticizes a girl in front of others or behind her back, or who makes offensive remarks.

After you've arranged a date with that cute girl from school, the evening will go more smoothly if you know how girls expect boys to act on a date. By following a few simple rules, you'll make a good first impression and have a good chance of getting another date.

First, when you go to pick up your date, be on time. The girl should greet you at the door, but if she doesn't, introduce yourself to the person who lets you in. What do you talk about with her parents while you're waiting for her to appear? Talk about any topic of general interest—sports events, a news item, a TV program, even schoolwork or the weather.

If the girl has a time-to-be-home rule, her parents will appreciate hearing you say, "I'll have Mary home by 11:00." Naturally, they'll expect you to keep your word.

A girl expects courtesy from a boy. She likes it when a boy holds open a car door or a room door for her. Another sign of good manners is to rise to your feet when a girl, woman, or older person enters a room, and to remain standing until they sit down. A girl will also expect you to help her into her coat, help her out of it, and hang it up for her.

One dating worry a boy sometimes has is how to keep the conversation going. What subjects does he talk about to a girl? Just about anything, really, but the conversation can be kept humming by using the interested question method. How

is she doing in the new math course? What are her vacation plans? Did she like a recent movie or new book? Her answers will suggest other subjects. That dead silence you're afraid might happen, doesn't.

When the date is over, a boy always thanks a girl by saying something like, "Thanks for going with me, it was fun." If he wants another date with her he can ask her then, or just say, "I'll call you, soon."

After the date is over

Boys often wonder if they should, or are supposed to, kiss a girl goodnight. Even though girls want to feel they're kissable, most agree they hope the boy doesn't try, especially on the first date. If he does, a girl thinks he probably tries to kiss every girl he dates. For this reason, a boy is smart to use the wait-and-see technique until he has dated a girl several times. By then she will have decided whether she wants him to kiss her goodnight, and he will know if he can try.

Sometimes, a couple never gets to the kissing stage, not because they don't like and enjoy each other, but simply because neither has any particular romantic feeling for the other. Not kissing doesn't spoil the fun of being together for them.

One thing girls really hate is the kiss-and-tell type of boy. Some boys do a lot of bragging about how they made out with girls. Even if you're tempted to join in this group you would be wise not to. Girls have a way of finding out who said what.

Once in a while, you may find that you can't keep a date. When that happens, you owe the girl an explanation just as fast as you can get to a telephone. If you don't have a good reason for breaking the date or if you don't explain it, a girl feels stood up. That hurts. She has every right to (and probably will) turn you down the next time you ask her to go out.

Sometime you may get a last-minute phone call from a girl who says she has a sudden "headache." In such a case, try not to show you are angry or hurt, because she may really be feeling ill. However, if the same thing happens again, you are probably getting a brush-off.

With a little dating practice, most boys get over being afraid to ask for a date because they might get turned down. Most girls will be nice about saying why they can't accept, but if the one you've asked doesn't offer an explanation, don't sulk, or nag her to give you a reason. Accept her decision, and end the conversation quickly by saying, "Well, thank you, anyway." And don't let one refusal throw you—ask another girl.

If the same girl turns you down several times and never offers any kind of explanation, you can be pretty certain you just don't appeal to her. It's best to accept that fact. There are plenty of girls around, and one of them may be eager to have you ask her.

If, however, several girls turn you down, you should check on yourself. Are you well groomed, including clean hands and fingernails? Are you a neat dresser, and are your manners all they should be? What about the crowd you run around with, and the things they do? Girls can be pretty choosy about things like these. Maybe you need some self-improvement.

Then too, a boy can limit his chances of hearing "yes" by deciding he wants to date only the glamour girl type. He spends so much time concentrating on how to get a date with one of these that he overlooks the fact that a lot of less glamorous girls can be more interesting. Half the fun of dating is discovering that girls are like a collection of clocks—each one ticks differently. The dating years are a boy's chance to learn what it takes to get along with girls. Every date does not have to skyrocket into romance. Girls can be wonderful friends.

Double-dating

Sometimes young couples double-date. Splitting the costs with another boy can make the evening less expensive. Also, sometimes a boy feels more comfortable having others around on those first dates. If he wants to double though, he should talk about it with his date first, to find out if she agrees.

Double-dates can be a lot of fun, especially if all four like the same kind of entertainment. There are some pitfalls a boy should avoid, however. Don't keep the conversation exclusively male by talking too much with the other boy. The girls will be bored, and rightly so.

If you get trapped into a too-long conversation with the other girl, your date will feel left out. Be sure to direct an occasional smile or question to her; this assures her you haven't forgotten you're with her. And, if all the others are strangers to her, be particularly attentive until you can see she feels at ease with everyone.

Maybe conversation comes easily to you, or perhaps you play a pretty good guitar. If so, great. But when you are with

a group, don't insist on being the life of the party. Give the others a chance to shine, too. Also, if your friend's date is a girl you have just met, don't try to make a big hit with her. That is a sure way to collect enemies instead of friends.

Pros and cons of going steady

The question of going steady is one that comes up in every boy's social life sooner or later. A boy usually finds one girl he wants to date more than any other. He feels at ease with her, and they enjoy the same things. Best of all, she makes him feel ten feet tall. Should he ask her to go steady?

In a very practical way, going steady is easier on a boy's wallet. His girl is more willing to be satisfied with simple, inexpensive dates than a new girl might be. Also, she is apt to have him over to her house more often for an evening get-together instead of having him take her out on every date. Because she usually knows what his financial limits are, she is more understanding when he can't afford a really big evening out. Furthermore, it boosts a boy's pride to know his girl wants to be with him more than she wants to go to expensive places.

Sometimes a boy has a broader social life when he goes steady. His girl expects him to escort her to whatever is going on, so he gets to a lot of social activities he might otherwise miss. Often, a boy acquires new interests, simply because his girl enjoys things like photography, dancing, ceramics, or something else he has never done.

Another thing in favor of going steady is that it eliminates digging up the courage to ask a new girl out for the first time. A boy knows where he stands with his own girl, and that is a comfortable feeling.

Going steady, however, does not guarantee that there will not be a breakup. Having that special girl tell you she no longer feels you are the "one and only" for her can hurt. It

can be a much bigger blow to a boy's pride than having a girl say "no" to a date.

And, the boy who decides to go steady often finds that the idea loses its rosy glow. Although it may make him feel great to be "needed" by his steady, his girl may be very possessive, and demand that the boy spend all his time with her. Most boys in the early dating years are not ready to abandon their old friends, or the all-male things they want him to do.

Even when a boy thinks he is old enough to go steady, he may find that he outgrows his girl. That cute little clinging vine he asked to go steady under a June moon may seem like an empty-headed doll in September. Nothing she says interests him anymore, and being together is no longer any fun for him. He feels trapped, and has an added problem—how does he tell her the bad news?

The biggest reason against going steady is that the teen years are the best chance a boy will ever have to find out what makes girls tick. What and how much he learns about girls are more important than he realizes for his later, adult stage of knowing how to get along with women. Men who say, "I'll never understand women," were often the boys who did not use their teen years learning how to get along with a lot of different girls.

Between that hard-to-ask-for first date and reaching the-big-man-on-campus status, exploring the new world of girls and dates can be fun. Just like driving a car, you learn by doing, and your dating skill improves with practice.

20

NECKING, PETTING, AND SEXUAL FEELINGS

In the years between 10 and 20, boys and girls start in earnest to have sexual feelings. The most immediate effects of these feelings are pure and simple physical reactions.

Girls and boys in these years usually feel all kinds of wonderful thrills and chills because they are becoming alive sexually. They have gradually, or possible suddenly, moved into a new world where holding hands, kissing, necking, and petting are exciting but somewhat frightening possibilities. Many times they do not know what to do because the feelings are strange and unfamiliar—but they want to do *something*.

Most people know what to do in familiar situations. They have learned how to act because they have been in similar situations. But when a person faces a new experience, he may not know what to do. His body may react in one way and his mind in another. Conflict occurs in many areas of life, but it is often more intense in sexual feelings. This is especially true among young people.

Sexual development

Around the time of puberty, a boy begins to develop whiskers on his face. At first there is a soft fuzz over his lip, and later it appears on his cheeks. New hair is growing on other parts of his body, too. It begins to grow first under his arms. Later, pubic hair begins to grow around his penis. The boy's shoulders become broader and his body becomes more muscular. He knows that he is no longer a small child, he is on his way to becoming a man.

These are visible changes. But invisible changes are also taking place. The boy's sex glands are now beginning to function. They cause him to feel less like a child. Before puberty, he may not have been interested in girls. In fact, he probably disliked girls. Now, his attitude begins to change. He may admit that not all girls are so bad; a few are really nice to be around. Before long, he discovers that he very much enjoys being around girls he likes.

310

As time goes by, the boy notices that just thinking about girls is sometimes enough to make him feel good all over. Such thoughts may cause his penis to stiffen. This stiffening is called an *erection*. While he probably had an occasional erection before puberty, he now realizes that this stiffening has something to do with his thoughts of girls.

All these things are normal and natural. They happen to every boy once he reaches puberty. But sexual feelings are nonetheless new to him. He may be—and probably is—not sure what to do about these new feelings.

As a girl nears puberty, she also begins to change. She has, of course, been growing since birth. But now the first signs appear that she is becoming a young woman. Her hips begin to widen, and her breasts begin to bud. Pubic hair starts to

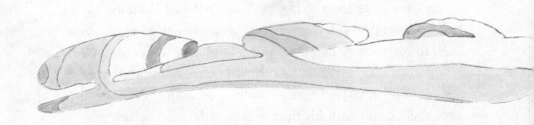

grow at the base of her abdomen, around her genital area. About six months later, hair also appears under her arms. In another six months or so, she has her first *menstruation*. When a girl menstruates for the first time, she knows that she is now or soon will be capable of giving birth to a child.

A girl is just as excited at the thought of becoming a woman as a boy is at the thought of becoming a man. And just as a boy's attitude toward girls changes, so does a girl's attitude toward boys change. She enjoys being around boys she likes, and she enjoys dating. The girl also becomes aware that part of the pleasant glow she has when she thinks about boys is due to her developing sexual feelings. These feelings are an indication that she is moving toward adulthood. But because such feelings are new to her, she may also be disturbed by them.

Dating—a path toward maturity

When boys and girls begin to date they are a bit afraid of each other. Being with a member of the opposite sex is a new experience for most of them.

Fortunately, boys and girls do not have to start out with single dating. Group activities such as parties and picnics usually are the first forms of dating. Group activities allow

312

boys to get to know something about what girls are like, and girls get to know something about boys.

As both the boys and girls develop more social confidence, they begin to meet in smaller groups. Three or four couples may go to a school basketball game. Double dating is the next step. Two couples might go to a movie together. Finally comes single dating. Both the boy and girl are more confident that they know how to act on a date.

Boys and girls together

Much of the fun of dating is purely social. Many couples do go out just to enjoy themselves. But simply having a good time dancing, bowling, or going to the movies are not the only reason why young people date. A boy and a girl date because they like each other. Each one likes to be with the other.

When they are not together, they enjoy thinking about the other person.

For a while after puberty, neither the boy nor the girl may be fully aware of the cause of these pleasurable feelings. The two of them may consider themselves just friends. They may feel that their friendship is not much different than the friendships they have had with members of their own sex.

But before long the boy and girl realize that their friendship is somehow different from anything they have known before. The sweet, soft glow they get when thinking of each other is something new. Eventually, each will understand that it is a new kind of feeling. The feeling may or may not be love.

Of course, a boy or a girl does not fall in love with the first person he or she dates. Far from it. But the ability to

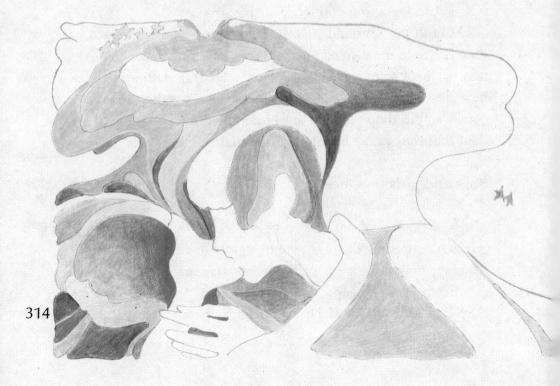

love is developing. At puberty a person is not physically an adult—he or she is becoming an adult. Similarly, young people are not yet emotionally ready for adult love when they first begin dating. It takes time to develop the capacity for adult love.

Still, after dating for a while, a boy and girl may wonder about the feelings they have for one another. Is it love? If it isn't love, what is it? How can I know whether it's love if I've never been in love before? What are these feelings that I feel? How can I express them? How *should* I express them?

It does not take long for the boy and the girl to recognize that there is a physical attraction between them. The boy very much wants to be close to the girl. He likes to hold her hand, and, though he may feel awkward at first, he wants to kiss the girl. Similarly, the girl also likes being close to the boy. Although she is unsure about how to act, she is pretty sure she would like to be kissed.

As the friendship between the boy and girl develops, both feel a growing urge to show their affection. They may begin holding hands on a date. The first goodnight kiss at the end of a date is a thrilling moment. As the boy and girl continue to date, there will be more kisses on other dates.

If one kiss was all there was to sexual feelings, there would be little conflict and confusion. But one kiss often leads to many kisses, especially if the boy and girl are very attracted to each other.

Before puberty a kiss is one thing. After puberty a kiss is something quite different. Both the boy and girl are moving toward adulthood. Because they are becoming sexually mature, kisses can cause them to become sexually aroused.

The nature of sexual feelings

The sexual drive is one of the most powerful feelings a human being can experience. In nature, the primary purpose of sex is reproduction. If human beings had no sexual feelings, none of us would be alive today, and no future generations would be born.

In this respect, human beings have something in common with animals. Animals, too, have powerful sexual drives which cause them to reproduce, thus carrying on the life cycle.

But there are many important differences between animals and human beings. One of the most important of these differences is that in animals reproduction is the *only* purpose of the sex drive.

Animals have no control over their sexual drives. Animals mate when their natural instinct tells them to. Human beings, on the other hand, are not creatures totally controlled by instinct. Human sexual feelings are not based solely on the need to reproduce. A man and a woman can have sexual feelings toward one another at any time. A married couple has sexual intercourse primarily because of the joy and pleasure it brings to each partner. It is an act of love. The woman does not become pregnant every time she has intercourse with her husband. Similarly, when two young people kiss each other goodnight after a date, the kiss is mostly a sign of affection, not a sign of an urge to have intercourse.

A second major difference between the sexual drives of human beings is that humans have some control over their sexual feelings. When a male animal is aroused, he will mate with any female he finds. During the mating season, a female will accept almost any male.

Human beings have the freedom of choice. A man and a woman do not marry because of instinct, but because they love each other. When a boy and a girl decide to date, they do so because they enjoy each other's company, not solely because of sexual feelings.

A third major difference between animals and human beings is that as soon as animals are physically able to reproduce, they usually do. It is not unusual for a female dog to have her first litter of puppies when she is only a year old. Even though she is still a young dog herself, she is able to take care of her puppies. She feeds them and protects them for a few weeks, and soon the puppies are ready to take care of themselves.

Human beings have responsibilities toward their children that no animal ever does. A human baby cannot take care of himself for a long time. Both the husband and wife must look after their child for many years. They must see to it that their child has a good home, adequate food, clothing, medical care, schooling, and many other things.

Ready but not ready—now what?

Although young people are physically able to become parents while they are still teenagers, they are not yet ready to take on the responsibilities of marriage. Nevertheless, they are beginning to have the same strong sexual feelings they will know when they are married.

A couple who have dated for a while may very much want to express their affection for each other. They may hold hands.

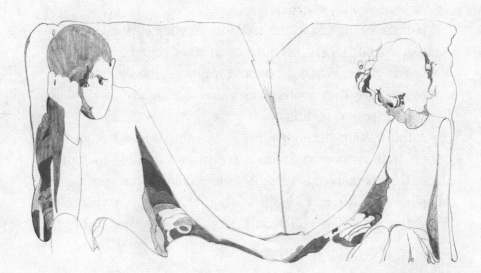

They may kiss each other. Or they may go further; they may *neck* or *pet*. When a boy and girl neck, they sit close together with their arms around one another and kiss. This is as far as they go. Petting also involves hugging and kissing, but it goes further, to touching and caressing the breasts and the genitals. These organs are the most sexually sensitive parts of the body. Petting almost always leads to sexual arousal. The boy has an erection. The girl becomes sexually excited. Both may lose control over their bodies and want to have sexual intercourse.

If a couple does start petting, it does not always lead to sexual intercourse, but there is always conflict. If they are able to suppress their sexual feelings, they both feel frustrated. If they are not able to suppress their feelings and have sexual intercourse, they both may feel sorrow and guilt.

When a husband and wife have intercourse, they are expressing their love for each other. This love is the result of their friendship, respect, and mutual understanding.

Their love probably grew slowly. They dated for a long time before becoming engaged. During that period, they had time to get to know one another well, not just as two people who simply wanted to satisfy their sexual feelings, but as two human beings. When they finally decided to marry, they knew what they were doing. They were ready to express their love through sexual intercourse, and they were ready to care for children they might have.

But when young people not yet ready for marriage become sexually aroused and have intercourse, they are most likely satisfying only their bodies. They have not yet had the time to learn the fullness of adult love. Sexual intercourse, which can be a deeply moving experience, may be nothing

more than "going all the way." The lack of emotion or love produces a hollowness and emptiness in sexual intercourse when only two bodies—and not two human beings—are involved. Because a man and wife love each other, sexual intercourse is satisfying emotionally, as well as physically.

Having sexual intercourse outside of marriage violates the customs and moral teaching of almost every society and religion. These customs and teachings, which are the result of centuries of cultural experience, were not created to frustrate young, unmarried people. Rather, they arose to prevent the unhappiness that can result from unthinking actions.

Moral codes are not strict, inflexible, and blind rules that are imposed to prevent people from doing this or that. They are signposts along the road—speed limit signs placed at dangerous points. Although the signs may not prevent someone from going too fast, they can warn of the dangers of speeding ahead without stopping to think of the possible results.

Even though sexual feelings can be extremely strong, each human being has the ability to keep these feelings under control. Each person has the power to decide how he will act and what he will do. He may use his body and his mind wisely and find happiness and fulfillment; but if he acts without thinking, he may bring unhappiness to himself and others.

Masturbation

When a boy becomes sexually mature, he develops strong sexual feelings. He is easily aroused. Sometimes simply thinking about girls may cause him to have an erection.

A boy or man does not ejaculate every time he has an erection. But if he is aroused, he may feel a stronger and stronger need to satisfy his sexual desire. He may ejaculate without having intercourse.

Even before puberty, children learn that they can stimulate their own genitals to produce a pleasurable feeling. After puberty, a boy learns that he can bring about ejaculation by handling his own genitals. This act is called masturbation. Just about every boy masturbates at some time or other while he is growing up. Many girls also masturbate.

While masturbation brings a certain amount of pleasure and relief from sexual tension, it may also cause conflict in the mind of the person who does it. Masturbation causes absolutely no physical harm. But because many people consider it wrong, a person who masturbates may feel guilty.

321

Although it may bring relief, masturbation is never completely satisfying. Even a person who masturbates frequently eventually recognizes that daydreams and fantasies are no substitutes for real life.

Homosexuality

A homosexual is a person who is sexually attracted to persons of the same sex rather than to persons of the opposite sex. One of the problems that masturbation can cause is that a young person may wonder if something is wrong with him or her. Some young people think that masturbation is linked to homosexuality. They believe that if they masturbate, they are a homosexual or will become homosexual. They should realize that masturbation does not cause homosexuality.

The sexual experimentation that goes on between boys and boys and girls and girls during childhood and adolescence also often makes them wonder if they are homosexual. This worry is needless in most cases. Sexual experimentation among people of the same sex at this age is normal. But this experimentation is usually only temporary. The vast majority of young people develop normal sexual tendencies and a good relationship with the opposite sex as they grow older.

What each should know

Although the sexual feelings that both young men and young women experience are similar, there are some differences. Misunderstandings can occur between two young people if they are not aware of and accepting of these differences.

By the time a boy begins dating regularly, he is probably

well aware of how strong his sexual feelings can be. The boy must keep in mind that he is likely to become sexually excited much more quickly and intensely than a girl. He must also recognize that his date may not fully understand the sudden, intense nature of his sexual feelings. She may not be ready or willing to respond to his advances. Knowing these things, the boy has a responsibility both to himself and to his date to keep his actions within limits.

The girl has responsibilities, too. She may enjoy flirting with a boy, but she must recognize that what she considers innocent flirting may set in motion overwhelming sexual desires in the boy. It is not completely up to the boy to make sure that things do not get out of control. Nor should the girl forget that she may also get carried away. Although a girl does not usually become sexually aroused as quickly as a boy, once she does become aroused, her feelings are every bit as intense and powerful as the boy's.

As the friendship between a boy and a girl grows, each has an obligation to respect the other's feelings and morals. They have an equal responsibility to set sensible limits and to stay within these limits. They must both learn that there is much more to a satisfying relationship than sex. Sex alone can never bring happiness if friendship, respect, and mutual understanding are absent.

21

PARENTS WATCH THE CLOCK

You are growing up. You are making more decisions for yourself and taking on more responsibilities. You may even be earning some money of your own.

Your parents see that you are developing a sense of responsibility. Even though they know that you are no longer a little child, they will still have obligations toward you until you are an adult and living on your own.

Parents want to protect you from anything that could injure your health or growth, be it physical, mental, or emotional. They want to steer you away from anything that might spoil your future, or cause you to drop out of school.

Until a few years ago, most of your activities were centered around your home. Now you are getting into more outside activities without your parents' presence. Parents have a natural concern about you when you are away from home and they are not able to protect you.

When parents worry about things happening to you, it is not because they doubt that you are capable of taking care of yourself. They caution you and make rules for your behavior because they know what is going on in the world around you. They know that many dangers exist, not only through their own experience, but because they read about these matters in the newspapers every day. Watch the headlines yourself. Many young persons do become involved in accidents, alcoholism, drug addiction, unwanted pregnancy, and disease. While you may believe, "This can't happen to me," your parents know there is a chance that it can. They will warn you repeatedly about their concerns because they love you.

What parents worry about

One of your parents' major anxieties when you are out is *automobile safety*. While you may not be old enough yet to have a driver's license, some of your older friends or an older brother or sister may be driving now. And the day will come when you will be old enough to get a license. Parents are concerned about young people driving because the number of persons under the age of 20 involved in auto accidents in the United States is frightening. According to the National Safety Council, 4,400,000 persons under the age of 20 were involved in accidents in 1968. Of that number, 10,500 of those young persons were killed, abruptly ending their lives tragically.

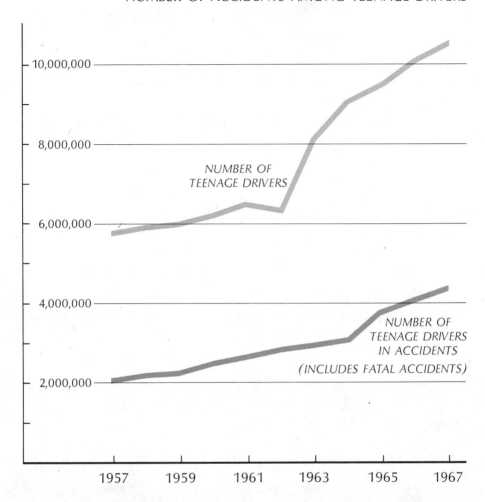

Insurance companies are very much aware of the problem. Because so many young persons are involved in accidents, insurance companies usually raise parents' rates when a young driver is added to the policy.

Because *liquor* slows down one's reactions, or gives a false feeling of courage, parents also worry about your drinking liquor and then going in an automobile. They will warn you repeatedly not to ride with a driver who has been drinking.

327

Parents read and hear about young people playing games with cars, playing "chicken" or having drag races. Misuse of an automobile is often the direct cause of an accident, and your parents will warn you against taking part in any of these often fatal games.

Your parents probably have talked to you about *smoking*. No doubt you have seen the advertisements on television warning of the possibility of cigarettes causing cancer and heart disease. The cigarette manufacturers have been required to print labels on their packages warning of the possible dangers of smoking. Your parents do not want you to develop a potentially harmful habit that you will find difficult to break. Your parents may have had the experience themselves of trying to stop smoking.

Your parents know of the existence of drug abuse. Harmful *drugs* are available near many schools. There are headlines in

the daily newspapers about police raiding "pot parties" or about arrests of peddlers on school grounds for selling marijuana to young people.

Parents will constantly warn you against trying a drug for "kicks," and they hope you will have the resistance to say no if you are faced with someone selling a drug or someone urging you to try it. Parents know that drug use can take many forms. Some youngsters begin with sniffing airplane glue to get a light and airy feeling. Some teenagers smoke "pot," or marijuana cigarettes. Some college students take another kind of drug to stay awake to study before examination time. Others use a form of sleeping pill in combination with other drugs to get an uplifted feeling. Youngsters who have had experiences with various drugs may begin to use heroin, an extremely dangerous and habit-forming drug.

Many young people have experimented with LSD. You probably have heard about LSD "trips." These are the feelings drug users have after taking the drug. In some cases, mental damage and even death follow such "trips."

Because drugs are illegal, they are usually expensive. Many young people who have become addicted to drugs have been forced to steal to get the money they need to buy drugs. Girls have been forced into prostitution, as well as theft. Many of these young people end up as criminals, and ruin their lives before they even have a chance to get started.

Your parents probably allow you to plan your own parties, to decide whether to play records or watch television, and to plan menus for refreshments yourself. But when it comes to *movies,* they are probably strict about which ones you may attend. Movies are vastly different now from what they were years ago. Until recently, almost all movies were designed to be entertainment for the entire family.

In recent years, however, many movies are made for shock value or have adult themes. Subjects that were forbidden on the screen several years ago are now being shown in neighborhood theaters. Homosexuality, sex relationships outside of marriage, and extreme violence are some of the themes made into movies for adult audiences.

In order to help parents decide what movies their children should see, the motion picture industry began rating movies for audiences in 1968. Newspaper advertisements for movies now carry either a *G, M, R,* or *X* rating. Your parents will probably only permit you to attend movies with a *G* rating, because these movies are intended for general audiences. Movies with an *M* rating are for mature audiences. An *R* rating means that persons under 16 will not be admitted to the theater unless accompanied by a parent or adult guardian. Movies marked *X* are intended for adults only; persons under 16 are not admitted, even if they are with a parent. In some cities the age limit for *R* and *X* movies may be higher than 16.

Parents worry about young people becoming involved in *sexual relationships* before they are old enough to have a meaningful man-woman relationship. They will warn about some of the social problems that can arise among young people. Your parents will want you to know that the dangers are present and will encourage you to stay away from them.

THE GIRL UPSTAIRS
ADULTS ONLY—RATED "X"

More teenagers are infected by the *venereal diseases* called *gonorrhea* and *syphilis* than by tuberculosis, scarlet fever, hepatitis, and polio combined. Many people spread these diseases because they do not know how they are transmitted. They are transmitted by sexual contact, usually sexual intercourse, with a person who already has one of the diseases. These germs cannot be inhaled from the air and they are almost never transmitted through toilet seats, eating utensils, or drinking fountains.

The real danger in these diseases lies in the fact that the infected person may ignore the symptoms of gonorrhea and syphilis for too long. The heart, brain, spinal cord, skin, and reproductive organs may be badly damaged before the in-

331

fected person seeks medical treatment. These diseases are treatable, and in most cases curable.

A concern parents have for daughters, especially, is that they will become involved in a relationship with a young man that might lead to an *unwanted pregnancy*. Your parents will caution you when you begin to go out alone on dates. They will have fears about your going steady when you are older, because when a girl goes steady, there is more opportunity for being alone with the young man and sharing greater intimacy. Unwanted pregnancy is a very real worry for parents, because each year over 150,000 unmarried teenage girls become pregnant. A pregnancy at an early age forces a girl to drop out of school, and it changes her whole life, as well as that of her parents.

Two-way responsibility

While at times you may feel like saying, "Leave me alone; let me decide things for myself," consider how insecure and alone you would feel if your parents had no concern for you.

Your parents are not being overly cautious in setting guidelines for you. Wise parents know that family responsibility works both ways. As part of the family, you must work together to build a happy life for all family members.

Jim, a 7th grader, cooperates with his parents about the hours he keeps. On school nights, he must be in at a certain hour. On special occasions, he explains to his parents why he needs an extra hour. They usually understand, and allow it. He always phones if he is detained or cannot get home when expected. That way, he can enjoy activities away from home while following flexible rules based on mutual trust.

But Jim is not the only one following rules. His parents also tell him where they are going, and what time they expect to return. They phone if they are detained. This procedure gives Jim and his parents a feeling of trust in each other.

Although you may sometimes feel resentful against parents' setting rules for your activities, you may also reluctantly admit that these regulations have been real lifesavers at times. They may have helped you to draw back from activities you wanted to avoid but were afraid to refuse for fear of what your friends might say.

Dating and parents

Parents have different but often definite ideas about the age they think is proper for their children to begin dating. While you may not be interested in dating yet, you probably think ahead to the time when you will want to date. How will your parents know when you are ready to date?

You can show them that you are mature enough to date

by proving your sense of responsibility. A sense of responsibility is a basic part of being adult. Responsibility can be demonstrated in many ways. You can show it around the house. Help with chores like lawnmowing, shopping, cleaning, or dishwashing. When you start a job, do it well, and complete it. Do a good job with your schoolwork. Be on time for appointments. Always cancel appointments you can't keep.

Some time in the future, you and your parents will probably talk about how often and how late you may have dates. Most parents do not favor dates on school nights. When young people are out late on school nights, they find it hard to get up the next morning, and they do not do as well at school the next day. They may not get all the sleep they need. Boys and girls with a mature sense of responsibility know that their schoolwork comes first. Most realize that dating is best confined to weekends when they can get extra rest the next day.

But good rules made in the spirit of responsibility between parents and youngsters must be flexible. Sometimes special events are held during the week that a boy and girl would attend anyway, and they want to go together. Parents giving permission for week night activities will want to set definite time limits for these activities, and will ask that your schoolwork be finished before you go out.

Plan flexible rules together

When discussing dating hours with your parents, try to imagine yourself in their position. They will consider your age. Younger children are asked to get home earlier. They will consider your sense of responsibility. If you have shown responsibility in the past, they will be more flexible in setting

335

rules. Does the activity take place at a neighborhood movie or at a distant basketball game? Are others to be picked up and taken home along with you? Will you be going on public transportation? What time will the activity be over? How long will it take to have some refreshments?

With all of these factors determining the lateness of activities and dates, it is not possible to set any one definite homecoming hour to suit all individuals or all occasions.

If young people want to avoid having parents treat them like children, they should show maturity by returning home at the time promised. Maturity on the part of young people breeds confidence and trust on the part of their parents.

Telling parents that "other kids stay out later" is not a good argument. Neither you nor your parents honestly know how late other young people stay out. Even if some of your friends do stay out much later than you, it may be that their parents are not exercising proper control.

Help keep parents' eyes off the clock

You can keep your parents from watching the clock too closely if you use courtesy and common sense. Always be sure your parents know where you will be, who you will be with, and who the adults in charge of social events will be.

Do not be vague about who is driving and what time you will return. If your parents don't know what time a party will end, they may begin watching the clock and the front door before the party is even over. Have an understanding with your parents that when you are away from home you will phone them if anything comes up to cause concern.

As you get older and spend more time with friends outside of your home, you will find that your parents make fewer rules and that they make the old ones more flexible. You and your parents will become more relaxed about your activities when you trust each other. And, as you mature into an independent individual, you will continue that important close relationship with your parents.

22

HOW
DO YOU
KNOW WHEN
IT'S LOVE

Everyone at some time wants to know what love is all about. Everyone also wants to know more specifically, "How will I know when I'm *truly* in love?"

The fact is that you've already been in "love" many times and in many different ways, and you have more of these experiences ahead of you.

The development of a person's ability to love goes through many stages, just as physical development occurs in many stages. There are times when very little seems to be happening. At other times, the changes seem overwhelming.

339

Nobody becomes three feet taller overnight. *Your* growth proceeds at a pace that is normal and just right for *you*. Your emotional or love development proceeds the same way. Love is something you will grow into, not fall into, in your own unique but normal way.

You have already gone through some of the stages of love development. You have already gone through self-love, love of mother and father, and love of other family members. You have reached beyond the family and shared the love of good friends. Sometime in the future you will find yourself attracted to many more persons and experience other forms of love.

You will probably have many crushes. Sometimes people call this *puppy love*. It is a kind of training period for the real thing, a phase of growing up. These stages are all in preparation for the mature love shared by a man and woman, and the lasting companionship of marriage.

Self-love and love of family

As a little baby you didn't know that there was anyone other than yourself to love. You were busy discovering your fingers, wiggling your legs, and listening to the funny noises you were learning to make. You came first, especially when you were hungry. Then everybody had to snap to attention to take care of you. This kind of love is self-love. It may remind you of some of your classmates and friends who seem interested only in themselves and in what others can do for them. You probably say that they are conceited. Perhaps they never completely outgrew the stage of self-love.

Most people do outgrow this stage, however, and begin to appreciate and love others. A baby usually has a special feel-

ing for his mother first. She is the one who provides him with
most of the comfort and attention he needs in the early months
of life. This love between mother and baby is sometimes so
strong that neither one ever really gets over it completely.
Again this may remind you of some of your friends, who even
now are so attached to their mothers that people may refer
to them as a "mama's boy" or "mama's little girl."

Usually, however, a baby begins to recognize and love the
strong arms and deep voice of his father, too. This love of
father often makes little girls want to imitate their mothers,
for they see how much father cares for mother. They think of
themselves as "little mothers" as they play with their dolls,
and they tell everyone quite seriously that when they grow up
they plan to marry their fathers.

Father has a big influence on young boys, too. Their love
for father makes them want to imitate the things he does. They

think they want to be just like him when they grow up. This probably includes marrying some one like mother — just as father did.

Learning to love the mother and then the father is an important stage in the development of a young child. It prepares him for the other loves in his life.

As a young child you found that your feelings of love could include others in your family. You developed affection for an older brother or sister that you could look up to, and count on for help. If you are the oldest child in the family, you have a younger brother or sister that you help and who is important to you, even if you do fight sometimes. This kind of love is very different from your earlier loves, for now you are giving as well as receiving.

Learning to love others

At last, having established some feelings of love for your family, you became brave enough to try relationships with "outsiders." These were probably other children in your neighborhood, both boys and girls about your own age. While you liked most of your playmates, there were probably one or two you thought were special. You preferred to spend more time with them than with others.

These first loves outside your family were more important than you may realize. Without them you might be dependent only on your family as a means for giving and receiving love.

As you grew older, your circle of friends widened. Perhaps some of these first loves are still among your present friends. But even now, you probably have one special friend of your own sex with whom you'd rather spend most or all of your time, someone you feel entirely comfortable with, to whom you can tell anything, whom you enjoy. You may argue and quarrel now and then, but you also make up. And this too is another special kind of love.

All of these love experiences, with members of your family, playmates, and close friends, are steps preparing you for the next stages of love involving members of the opposite sex.

Perhaps you already attend boy-girl parties or other group activities like picnics and dances. If not, they will begin for you someday. A short while later, these parties will become the type where a boy or a girl will ask someone to come as his or her date. You will then have entered yet another stage in your love development.

Perhaps this development does not yet appeal to you. The age at which boys and girls get over their disinterest—or even dislike—of members of the opposite sex varies widely. However, it can be very exciting when you discover how interesting the opposite sex is!

Girls suddenly find that boys are an interesting topic of conversation. Girls become interested not only in talking about boys, but also in talking with them. They even some-

times find themselves dreaming about boys. The idea of romantic love begins to appeal to them. The same kinds of things happen to boys.

If your feelings have not reached this point yet, do not be worried or unhappy. You have plenty of time for these experiences. When you are truly ready for them, you will know it, and you will enjoy them much more when they come naturally than if you feel forced into them.

As young people move into their teen years and increase the number of their boy-girl experiences, they find that the intensity of these experiences increases. The idea of romantic love, as shown in movies and television, can sometimes confuse them. On the screen, when the hero and heroine meet, take one look at each other, and fall into each other's arms, the audience knows it's "love at first sight."

You may dream of something like this happening to you. But in the real world, love doesn't often happen this way. It is true that you may be instantly attracted to someone—you just like the way he or she looks or speaks—but love is much more than an instant attraction. Your previous experiences have taught you there are many ingredients necessary in loving someone. Coming to love someone is much more complicated than a look, a sigh, and an embrace.

Falling in love again . . . and again

The feelings you may have after just one look at an attractive stranger can be very powerful, however. These sudden feelings can be called *crushes,* or *infatuations.* A dictionary says that someone who is infatuated is "made foolish by love," or "blindly in love." The very suddenness of the feeling is a kind

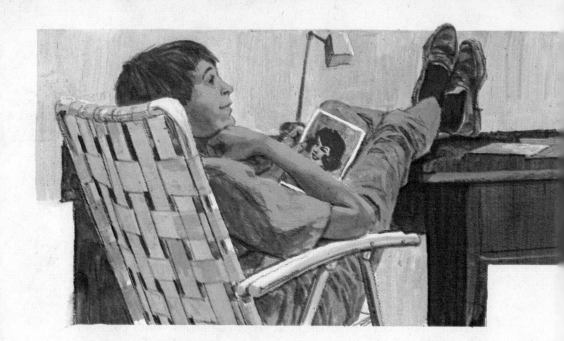

of warning. There are many possible reasons for such an instant attraction. Two of these reasons are most common.

The first reason is physical attraction. The other person's smile makes you want to smile, too (maybe even grin foolishly), and the whole world seems to light up. Perhaps it's the way this person looks at you, or walks, or talks. Suddenly, you've fallen for him or her. It's a marvelous, very special feeling that you can't explain—but you hope it never ends.

Another possible cause for this "head over heels" feeling is meeting someone who makes you feel you've been friends all your life. That person may even remind you of someone very close (your mother, your father, a special aunt or uncle), although you may not realize at the time that that is the reason you're so attracted. All you know is that this is just the person you've dreamed of meeting, and at last the dream has come true.

In both of these kinds of crushes, one thing is important. You are being attracted to one aspect of the person you've

346

fallen for—not by the person as a whole. At the time this won't matter to you. You will probably be blinded by your feelings, and refuse to see the bad or weak qualities this person may have. You would be furious if anyone tried to tell you that there was something wrong with your "dream come true."

All that matters—and quite rightly at this stage in your development—is that you are happy with your partner of the moment. Those last three words are important in describing crushes, for they usually are short in duration.

Sometimes crushes happen during a summer vacation, and vanish with the first day of school. Sometimes crushes last longer, then, surprisingly, the intense feelings suddenly disappear one day with no warning at all. This is all very natural and common. And as quickly as these feelings disappeared, they can reappear at the sight of someone new.

With each new crush, you are likely to think, "This is it!" only to find after a short while that indeed it isn't, and you prepare yourself for the next experience. After a while this may become disappointing and disheartening. You might begin to think perhaps you will never find the person who's right for you. But don't be discouraged. This stage of on-again-off-again feelings, of being very mixed up, happens to everyone, and it is just as important as all the other stages in a person's love development.

If you realize that the powerful feelings of crushes are preparing you for yet another stage, you can learn a lot from some of your experiences. You will learn that a lasting love between two people needs more than physical attraction and a good conversation. Love may begin because of these things, but its development into more mature, lasting love comes as you learn to recognize other qualities in the person to whom you are attracted. It will be partly through your crushes that you will discover which qualities are most important to you.

Perhaps you are a quiet person who needs someone to draw you out and help you enjoy things. Or perhaps you are very frivolous and outgoing, and someone who offers a steadying hand is just right for you. It is only through trial and error that you will find these things out. It is for this reason that crushes, though sometimes heartbreaking when they end, are really an important stage in the development of a person's ability to love. As your emotions mature and you learn more about yourself and about why you love and are loved, the better able you will be to think wisely about choosing a life-long partner.

Someone to love and marry

You may wonder if you will survive all of these stages in your love development. You may wonder when you will get to the point where you can use the knowledge you have gained in making a choice and in accepting the responsibilities of really loving someone. At the proper time, a bit of each of your earlier stages of love development will fit into place and will help to prepare you for married love and family life. Someday you will develop a feeling for a person with whom you can share the many kinds of love.

Love is a complicated relationship, and like any good lasting relationship it requires generosity, self-control, imagination, and patience. When you take that big step into marriage, don't be misled into thinking that now you can just sit back and enjoy it. Great satisfaction will continue to come only if you continue to provide the necessary ingredients for success and share all the varied responsibilities. Among these responsibilities will, of course, be the birth of your own children. It is then that you will see for yourself the beginning stages of the love development that you went through as a baby and child.

23

WHAT
ABOUT
MARRIAGE

Marriage (mar' ij) *noun,* 1. *The state of living together as husband and wife.* 2. *The ceremony of being wed, of becoming man and wife.*

❀   ❀   ❀

You might wonder why anybody would want to look up a word like **marriage** in the dictionary. It is one of those words that everybody knows the meaning of, like *lock, bolt,* or *blue.* But if you think about these last three words, you will realize that each has more than one meaning. If you look these words up in a dictionary, you will find that they have additional meanings you may not have known about.

Marriage is also a word that has many meanings, and not simply dictionary meanings. Marriage has almost as many meanings as there are people who are married. In fact, it has about as many meanings as there are people in the world.

This sounds like a rather big claim. But is it? Suppose you were asked to write your own definition of the word. Aside from a dictionary-type definition, what would you say about marriage? What are your views and opinions? Whatever they are, you would probably agree that your idea of marriage differs, in some ways, from the ideas of your friends, your brothers and sisters, or your parents.

Some people know a lot about marriage; some know very little. Some think that marriage is the best thing that can happen in life; some think it is the worst. Some people feel that their life will not be complete if they do not marry; some believe that marriage is not necessary. Age, experience, and personal feelings all affect a person's concept of marriage. Obviously, *marriage* is not a word like *lock*. You cannot learn all there is to know about it by looking in the dictionary, or in any book for that matter.

Facts about marriage

There are some facts, however, that we can start with. First, *marriage is popular*. At some time in their lives, the majority of people want to get married, and do get married. About 75 percent of the population of the United States over 14 years of age is, or has been, married. Nine out of ten people who live to be 50 years old or older eventually marry, although it may be late in life. Although many people marry more than once in their lives, the majority of people marry only once.

People get married for a variety of reasons. Mutual love, of course, is one of the strongest reasons. But additional reasons also exist. A person may want to marry to become independent of his parents. He may want to be the head of a household and to have a home of his own. He may also want to have children. Other reasons include companionship, fulfillment of sexual desire, and emotional security. For a woman, marriage usually offers protection and economic security. For a man, marriage often offers social and business advantages.

In addition, people get married because they think they are expected to get married. Our society is not much different from other societies in this respect. Marriage is the founda-

tion for a stable society. Thus, young adults feel a social pressure to get married. Part of a person's social status depends on whether or not he is married. An unmarried man or woman is said to be "single." The implication is that being "single" is being in an unfinished, unfulfilled state of development . . . like being half of a pair of scissors.

One by one, a person's friends marry. Seeing one's friends marry becomes, in itself, a strong reason for marrying, especially for women. As more and more of his friends get married, a man finds that his social life changes. His married friends have new responsibilities and new interests. Their lives have changed. He no longer has the same kind of friend-ship with them. To him, it seems as though everyone is married or is getting married, so he also begins to think about finding a wife.

Some of the reasons for getting married are better than others. To marry for security, business advantages, or because everyone else seems to be getting married, are not in themselves good reasons. Before a person makes up his mind to marry, he must consider the responsibilities involved, and decide whether he is ready to accept these responsibilities.

When is a person ready for marriage?

Sometimes a young man or woman who wants to marry is told that he or she "is not old enough." The young person often refuses to accept this. He is sure that he *is* old enough. He often does not realize that age is not the only factor. Being old enough to marry means many different things.

First, the person must be old enough physically. Before puberty the sex organs of boys and girls are not fully developed and functioning. (Most people reach puberty between the ages of 12 and 14.) Boys and girls cannot become parents until they have passed puberty. Their bodies will continue growing physically until they are around 17 or 18 years of age. At 14 or even 17, few girls and even fewer boys are ready for marriage. Physically they are old enough. Emotionally and socially they are still developing.

As boys and girls become teenagers, they begin to take more of an interest in each other. They begin to have sexual feelings. A boy's feelings, however, differ from a girl's. A boy is more consciously interested in sex. He enjoys daydreaming

355

about sexual activities. As he begins to date regularly, he wants to have sexual experiences. He may or may not engage in premarital sexual intercourse, but he does think about sex. To the boy, sex and love are not necessarily the same thing. He is less likely than the girl to confuse the two feelings.

A girl, although sexually sensitive, is not usually as interested as a boy in physical sex. She is pleased with the attention paid to her by boys, but she feels that this interest is due to her personality and charm. Her daydreams are more likely to be about love than sex.

The boy has one attitude; the girl another. This difference in outlook often leads to misunderstandings. The boy sometimes does not understand the girl's behavior; she is equally confused by his. Both are beginning to bridge the gap in understanding, but neither fully understands the situation yet.

Teenage boys and girls are still largely wrapped up in themselves. Although he may be strongly interested in girls,

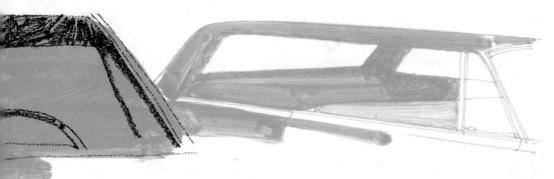

and she may be just as interested in boys, both of them are still most of all interested in themselves. The boy is the hero of his fantasies; the girl is the heroine of hers. Neither one is emotionally mature enough to be able to share his life in the way that marriage demands.

Dating helps teenagers to mature emotionally. By dating they learn to get along with members of the opposite sex. Boys begin to understand that girls have feelings, attitudes, and reactions different from their own. Girls learn the same about boys. Members of both sexes start to develop realistic views in place of fantasies. Girls daydream less and less about a tall, dark, and handsome prince. Boys daydream less and less about adventures with beautiful women. A boy decides what qualities he wants in a girl. A girl decides what type of boy she likes. As a result, dating becomes more selective. Eventually, marriage is the result.

The differences between infatuation and love

How long does all this take? How long is it from a person's first date to his wedding? How many different people must a person date before he finds his marriage partner?

Many young people see dating as a kind of trial-and-error experience. Somewhere out there is the Right Person. All they have to do is keep looking until they find him or her. They sometimes even believe that they might find the one love of their life overnight.

It is not quite as simple as that. Problems arise. A person who is not yet emotionally mature is still too much concerned with himself. He falls in love easily, but falls out of love just as easily. He confuses **infatuation** with **love**. The two may appear to be similar, and at this stage in his emotional growth it is very difficult for him to tell them apart.

A person may think he is in love simply because he wants to be in love. But wanting to be in love and being in love are two different things. Infatuation, not love, is likely to be the result. What is the difference? Infatuation, like popcorn, instantly and suddenly develops. Love, like an ear of corn, takes time to grow. A person who is infatuated will see only the

positive qualities of that person. A person in love can see both the good qualities and at least some of the less-than-good qualities in the person he loves.

It is possible to be infatuated with more than one person at a time. A boy may honestly feel that he is very much in love with two different girls. Each girl has different qualities that appeal to him. He spends a good part of his time wishing that somehow all the qualities he likes could be combined into one girl. He often finds a third girl who appears to have all these qualities, at first, anyway. But then he meets a fourth girl. . . .

Genuine love is a more constant thing. A person directs most of his love toward someone else. He is emotionally mature enough to be able to care about someone else first, and himself second. The infatuated person is primarily concerned only with himself.

How can you know if what you feel is love, not just infatuation? How can you be sure that you are old enough, in all senses, to marry? You can never be completely sure. Doubts always creep in. At some time in your life you have probably thought of yourself as the greatest person who ever lived. Yet at other times, you might have felt that you cannot do anything right, that you are a complete failure. Everyone has oc-

casional doubts about his own personal worth. But such doubts, although generally baseless, are not totally bad.

When a person seriously begins to consider marriage, it is better in the long run if he does have a few doubts. These doubts are the beginnings of sound judgment. A person who is convinced he is the greatest person in the world *is* the greatest person in *his own* world. He must realize that marriage will double the population of his world.

Maturity and responsibilities of marriage

By questioning whether he is in love, or is mature, or is old enough to marry, a person is probing, testing, and analyzing. The mature person is not afraid to ask questions, nor is he afraid of the answers, even if they are not always the answers he would like to hear. The real world is much less certain than the world of daydreams. But the rewards of the real world are much more satisfying than those of any daydream.

The mature person faces reality, pleasant or unpleasant. He recognizes that the world is very large indeed, and he attempts to adjust to living in it as best he can. He knows that it is useless to try to run away from what is. As a person matures, he sees that nothing stays the same: everything, and everyone, changes. What seems to be a terrible problem today may not be so tomorrow.

A mature individual is wise enough to trust his own judgement as well as doubt it. He has developed the confidence to do both. When he thinks about getting married, he knows that there is more to marriage than love alone. There are financial obligations, for example. Marriage means setting up a home, even if it is simply a two-room apartment. Can he af-

ford to get married now? If he is still in school, should he
marry before he completes his education? Will he be earning
enough to raise children in the surroundings they will need for
healthy growth?

Another factor a young man or woman must consider before marriage is social maturity. Each person must think about
how marriage will change his or her life. Before marriage an
individual usually has a good deal of personal freedom. If he
lives at home, his parents pay the bills of the household. If he
lives by himself or with roommates, he will have to pay for
rent and food, but he is still fairly free to do what he wants
when he wants to. The money he earns is his own. He is independent; he is single.

When a man and woman marry, neither is single any
more. The husband can no longer think of the money he

earns as entirely his own. He can no longer spend it as only he pleases. His wife has a right to a share of it for her personal use and for buying food, clothing, furniture, and so on. If his wife has a job, part of what she earns will also go to her husband.

Saving money for a home and a family is important, too. Both husband and wife may have to adjust to spending less on entertainment and luxuries. Money a single person might have spent on a new stereo or sportscar may have to go for a new carpet or a more family-type car.

The wife must be ready and able to accept the responsibilities of running her own household: cleaning, preparing meals, doing the wash, budgeting the household money, and many other "unromantic" things of this kind. In addition, she must think ahead to having children and raising a family.

Before anyone marries, he or she must be mature enough to recognize that marriage is often hard work. Marriage is

not all joy and happiness, even though the hard work can be less difficult when it is shared. The couple should not expect other people, their parents for example, to solve their problems for them. They must have the confidence to rely on themselves when things go wrong.

Day-to-day living together as man and wife can seem unglamorous. Yet, in spite of the responsibility, the work, and the loss of personal freedom, most people do get married—and enjoy being married. Marriage is the normal and most satisfactory way of expressing adult love. Happily married men and women see the duties of marriage as part of their adult responsibilities. They accept these duties and take pride in their responsibilities. Marriage is both a challenge and an achievement.

Selecting a husband or wife

When you feel you are ready for marriage, whom do you marry? Dating helps a young person find the answer to this question. By dating several girls over a long period of time, a young man begins to form an idea of the kind of girl he likes best. Girls also decide what type of man they prefer through dating many young men.

Dating a person, even **going steady,** is not the same as being married to that person. A boy or a girl who is great fun to be with on a date may still not be the right marriage part-

363

ner. Personal characteristics that are not apparent or are unimportant on a date may be very important in a marriage.

Suppose that a girl is attracted to a certain boy because of his devil-may-care attitude toward life. He dresses as he pleases. He spends all his money on clothes, on his car, and on her. He thinks of himself as free and independent. To the girl, the boy may seem to be a romantic and dashing figure. But would he be ready to take on the responsibilities of marriage? Would he be willing to accept the fact that marriage had taken away much of his independence?

Suppose that a boy is attracted to a certain girl because of her beauty and sense of humor. She is proud of her looks and spends a good deal of her time and money on clothing, hair styling, and make-up. She always has something witty to say,

364

and she seems to be interested in everything around her. About the only thing she does not seem to like is getting her hands dirty. This girl is also a romantic and attractive figure to the boy. But how would she act if she had to live on a small income? Would she feel that keeping house or caring for children was her proper role in life?

These are not typical examples, of course. But they do show that a person who might be great fun to date might not be a suitable partner for marriage. Furthermore, tastes and attitudes change. As young people grow older, they often look back at their earlier dating experiences with amusement and embarrassment: "How could I ever have seen anything in him!" "It's hard to believe that I ever dated her. . . ."

To avoid making a mistake in choosing a marriage partner, a person must rely on his head as well as his heart. Of course this does not mean carrying a list in your pocket of all the good qualities you want in a husband or wife and searching around until you find a person who has all of these qualities. Remember, nobody is perfect—including you, and also including the person you eventually choose to marry.

Before marrying, a person should think about the qualities of the person he loves that irritate him as well as the qualities he likes. This is not easy when one is in love, but it is important. Are the irritating things bothersome enough to lead to unhappiness? Or are they just minor faults? Suppose that the woman is very punctual. She is always on time wherever she goes. The man she is engaged to is less aware of time. He does not consider it "all that terrible to be late occasionally." How much does it bother the woman when he causes her to be late? How often is he "occasionally" late? Is it really that important to always be on time?

The woman must answer these questions for herself, before marrying. Perhaps she feels that she can change his habits after they are married. But what if she cannot? Few ever succeed. What if the man resents her efforts? He may not see punctuality as a great virtue. Instead, he may feel that the woman has an abnormal concern with always being on time. Will this minor irritation grow into a major marital problem? Or will the man and the woman learn to adjust to each other's differences?

Every marriage is different. One reason why is that every person in the world is different. Whom should you marry? That is up to you—and the person who wants to marry you! From what marriage counselors have learned about marriage,

however, it is safe to say that the person you marry will be like yourself in many ways. You will probably have common interests, common ideals and values, and similar backgrounds. Your level of intelligence will be about the same, as will the level of education you have. In fact, you will probably even be similar in size, give or take a few inches. The five-foot-two cheerleader rarely marries the six-foot-six basketball star. They just do not see eye to eye!

There will be differences between you, too. You may be interested in sports; your marriage partner may enjoy going to concerts. You may collect stamps as a hobby; the other person may prefer reading. Learning to accept and appreciate the ways you are different is necessary to make a marriage work. Differences can cause conflict, but they can also provide stimulation. To marry someone who has *exactly* the same interests as you do can sometimes fail to provide stimulation.

When you have thought as much as you can think about the complex business called marriage, you and your chosen partner will go ahead and marry. In spite of remaining fears and doubts, you will probably find that marriage is not all that frightening. Recognizing and taking pride in your maturity, accepting the obligations of life and society, and confident in your mutual love, the two of you will be ready to face the uncertainties of the future. Two single persons will have become a two-person team.